Donated by

SAN RAMON LIBRARY FOUNDATION
100 Montgomery • San Ramon • California 94583

# Mary Anning

# Mary Anning
## Fossil Hunter

WITHDRAWN

by Sally M. Walker
illustrations by Phyllis V. Saroff

On My Own

BIOGRAPHY

Carolrhoda Books, Inc./Minneapolis

The author wishes to express special thanks to Hugh Torrens for his time, good advice, and suggestions.

The photograph on page 46 appears courtesy of the Natural History Museum, London.

Carolrhoda Books, Inc.
A division of Lerner Publishing Group
241 First Avenue North
Minneapolis, MN 55401 U.S.A.

Website address: www.lernerbooks.com


Library of Congress Cataloging-in-Publication Data

Walker, Sally M.
    Mary Anning : Fossil hunter / by Sally M. Walker ; illustrations by Phyllis V. Saroff.
    p. cm. — (On my own biography)
    Summary: Describes the life of Mary Anning, who discovered many of the best and
  most complete fossils in nineteenth-century England, yet received little credit for her
  work.
    ISBN 1-57505-425-6 (hardcover)
    1. Anning, Mary, 1799–1847—Juvenile literature. 2. Anning, Mary,
1799–1847—Childhood and youth—Juvenile literature. 3. Women
paleontologists—England—Biography—Juvenile literature. [1. Anning, Mary,
1799–1847. 2. Paleontologists. 3. Women—Biography.] I. Saroff, Phyllis V., ill.
II. Title. III. Series.
QE707.A56 W35  2001
560'.92—dc21
    [B]                                                                              99–040094

Manufactured in the United States of America
1  2  3  4  5  6  –  SP  –  06  05  04  03  02  01

*For Shannon Zemlicka, an editor whose discerning eye helps me separate the wheat from the chaff*

—S.M.W.

*For my father, Harry A. Saroff*

—P.V.S.

*Lyme Regis, England*
*1809*

Ten-year-old Mary Anning walked
to the bottom of the cliff.
She turned over a rock,
then shook her head.
Her father and her brother, Joseph,
looked at rocks near the water.
Mary lifted her hammer.
She chipped at another rock.
A piece broke off.
Mary picked it up and smiled.
She had found another curiosity.

7

Mary's "curiosity" was really a fossil.

When animals die,

their bodies slowly break into pieces.

They become part of the earth.

Bones and shells

are left on the ground.

Soil and sand may cover them.

Over thousands of years,

they may turn to stone.

Then they are called fossils.

Plants can become fossils, too.

Even footprints can turn to stone.

Mary, Joseph, and their father
were fossil hunters.
The fossils they found
were of animals that lived
about two hundred million years ago.
Many were ammonites.
Ammonites were a type of shellfish.
They swam in the sea.
They had flat, coiled shells.

Mary's life was unusual
for a girl in the 1800s.
Most people thought girls
should not learn about fossils.
They didn't think girls
should learn about science at all.
Mary's father, Richard, did not agree.
He liked to take Mary and Joseph
on fossil hunts.

The Annings spent
many hours outdoors.
They walked along the beach.
They waded in the water
and climbed along
the bottom of the cliffs.
Wind, rain, waves, and frost
often made rocks fall
from the cliffs.
Some of those rocks
contained fossils.
Richard taught Mary and Joseph
to look carefully at the rocks.
He showed them
how to find fossils
and how to collect them.

The Annings liked fossil hunting.
But they didn't do it just for fun.
Richard Anning put the fossils
on a table in his furniture shop.
People who visited Lyme Regis
bought them.
The money helped the Annings
pay their bills.

When Mary was 11,
her father was hurt.
He fell off a cliff
on his way to a nearby town.
Richard was already sick at the time.
After his fall, he became weaker.
In October, he died.

Without Richard's furniture shop,
the Annings became poor.
Even worse, they owed a lot of money.
Finding and selling fossils
became very important.
Mary's mother took charge
of the fossil business.
Mary and Joseph helped.
The children searched the beaches,
even in cold, wet weather.
They knew that winter storms
made rocks fall from the cliffs.
Fossils were easier to find then.
Mary and Joseph had to be careful.
If rocks fell on them,
they could be hurt.
They might even be killed.

In 1811, Joseph found a skull.

It had a long snout and many teeth.

It looked like a crocodile.

Joseph told Mary where he had found it.

About a year later,

Mary found the rest of the fossil.

It was very big.

Mary could not chip it out of the cliff.

She and her mother
hired men from town.

They helped Mary remove the fossil.

Then they carried it to her house.

The Annings sold the fossil.
The man who bought it
gave it to a museum in London.
The scientists there were excited.
Here was a complete fossil
of a reptile that had lived in the sea!
They had never seen such a thing.
In 1817, they named the reptile
an ichthyosaur.

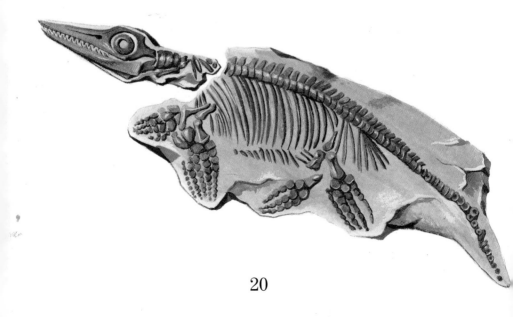

Selling the ichthyosaur

helped the Annings pay some bills.

But they were still poor.

Joseph wanted to earn more money.

He got a job learning to put covers

on furniture.

Mary kept collecting fossils.

By the summer of 1819,

the Annings needed money badly.

They had not found any large fossils

for almost a year.

Mary's mother had to pay the rent.

She was ready to sell

the family's furniture.

Then a man who collected fossils

decided to help.

Colonel Thomas Birch had often
bought fossils from the Annings.
He knew they had found
many of England's best fossils.
Colonel Birch was worried
that the Annings were so poor.
In 1820, he sold his collection.
He gave the money to Mary's mother.

The next year, the Annings discovered
another ichthyosaur.
A group of men bought it.
They gave it to a museum.
In those days,
museums did not give credit
to people who found and sold fossils.
They gave the credit to the people
who gave the fossils to the museum.
The men who bought the ichthyosaur
were listed in the museum's records.
But the Annings were not.

When Mary was 24,

she made another important find.

She discovered a plesiosaur fossil.

Like ichthyosaurs, these strange reptiles

had lived in the sea.

Mary's plesiosaur was nine feet long

and six feet wide.

Its mouth was filled with sharp teeth.

Its neck was long, like a snake.

Instead of legs, it had four flat paddles.

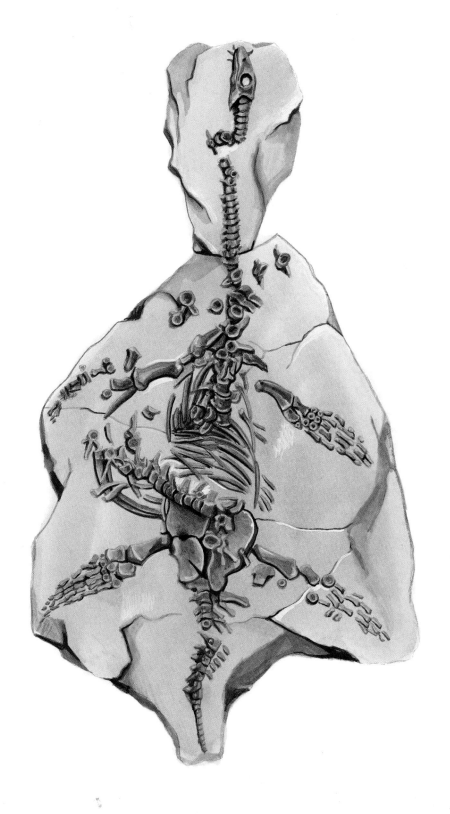

Until Mary's discovery,

only pieces of plesiosaurs had been found.

Scientists didn't know

exactly what they were.

Because Mary's fossil was

almost complete,

scientists learned something exciting.

Plesiosaurs belonged to a new genus,

or large group, of reptiles.

No one had known this

until Mary found her plesiosaur.

A famous scientist wrote a report

about Mary's fossil.

He did not mention Mary.

But people heard that she had found it.

Soon, visitors to Lyme Regis

wanted to meet Mary Anning.

Mary learned as much as she could
about the fossils she loved.
She studied other people's fossils.
The Philpot sisters had a big collection
in Lyme Regis.
They let Mary look at it.

Mary also wrote letters to scientists.

They sent her books and papers.

Mary compared what she read

with the fossils she found.

She also compared her fossils

with living sea animals.

She shared her ideas with the scientists.

Slowly, they began to respect her.

By 1825, Mary's brother, Joseph,
had left the fossil business.
Mary took charge.
Running a business was unusual work
for a woman in those days.
Hunting for fossils
was even more unusual.
Many people thought Mary was as odd
as the fossils she found.
Mary was odd in another way, too.
She liked to say what was on her mind.
Mary studied her fossils carefully.
She knew how their bones fit together.
If a scientist put bones together wrong,
she spoke up.
She was not afraid to disagree
when she knew she was right.

Every day, Mary hunted fossils.

Sometimes she walked 10 miles.

Her dog, Tray, often went with her.

Mary's hard work paid off.

In 1828, she found a belemnite.

Belemnites once lived in the sea.

Like squid, they could squirt
clouds of ink.

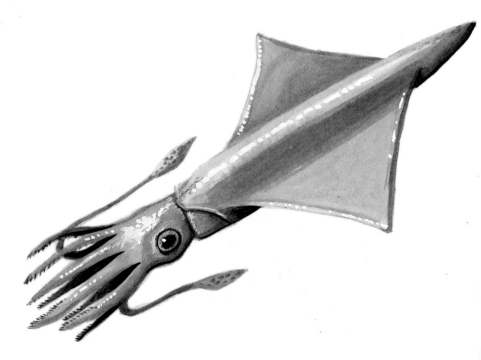

Mary had found belemnites before.

But this one was special.

Most fossils are formed from

bones or shells, not soft body parts.

Mary's fossil showed the outline

of the belemnite's soft ink sack.

It even contained some ink.

Later that year,

Mary found a pterosaur fossil.

Pterosaurs were reptiles with wings.

Mary's was the first found in England.

People were amazed by the fossil.

Had this creature really been alive?

It had teeth, hooked claws, and wings.

It looked like a flying dragon.

A scientist named William Buckland

described Mary's fossil in a report.

And he wrote that Mary had found it!

Mary's work was better known than ever.

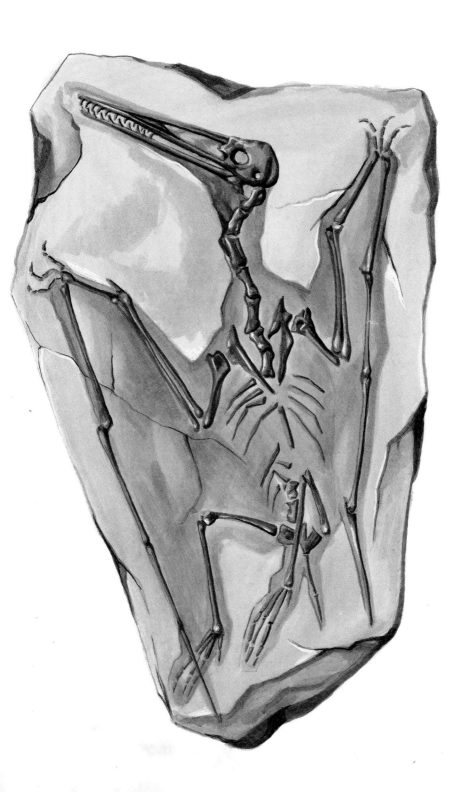

When Mary was collecting fossils,
she often lost track of time.
She did not always notice
what was happening around her.
One day in 1829,
Mary was removing a fossil from a cliff.
She was so busy
that she did not notice the water.
The tide was coming in fast.

Mary and her helper had to dash
through the water to safety.
They made it just in time.
Mary thought the danger was worth it.
The fossil she had found
turned out to be another plesiosaur.
It was even better than the first.

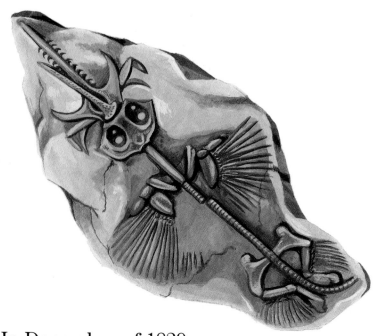

In December of 1829,

Mary found another strange fossil.

Its teeth were shaped like hooks.

The body had flaps, like wings.

The flaps reminded Mary of a stingray.

She cut open a stingray

to see if it looked like her fossil.

The bones were different.

Still, Mary thought the fossil was a fish.

Some scientists agreed with her.

Others thought it was a reptile or a bird.

Years later, scientists learned
Mary's fossil *was* a fish.

It was a chimaera.

Chimaeras have pointy snouts.

Their tails are long, like whips.

Just as Mary had thought,
they are related to stingrays.

In 1830, Mary found her third plesiosaur.

Over the next few years,

she found many small fossils, too.

And she had a close call in 1833.

She was searching

along the bottom of a cliff.

Tray was nearby.

Mary heard a rumbling sound.

Before she knew it,

a pile of rocks had fallen.

Tray was killed.

Mary was very upset.

But hunting fossils was her job.

She returned to the beach many times

to find more fossils.

Mary did well selling fossils.

She rented a house with a bigger shop.

She also gave money
to poor people who lived in Lyme Regis.

Many people visited her.

Mary liked to teach children
about her fossils.

She was glad to talk
with anyone who wanted to learn.

Mary died in 1847.
Long after she was gone,
people still studied her fossils.
They kept asking questions
about those strange animals.
Mary Anning did not get much credit
for the work she did.
But she never gave up hunting fossils.
Her fossils helped people learn
about life in the sea,
two hundred million years ago.

## Afterword

During Mary Anning's time, it was difficult for women to become scientists. Most universities were not open to women. Mary could not have afforded an education anyway. So she learned on her own by asking questions, reading, and studying fossils. Some of the people who bought fossils from Mary believed she knew more about them than anyone else in England.

In the past, Mary received little credit for her work. It was easy for the scientists of the 1800s to forget a woman who sold her fossils for money. In fact, many stories about Mary tell only about the ichthyosaur she found in 1812—and they don't always tell the truth.

But letters, journals, and scientific articles from Mary's time have helped us understand her contribution. The fossils Mary collected led people to many questions and answers about the history of Earth and its animals. Slowly we have begun to learn the truth about Mary Anning, a determined woman who became one of the greatest fossil hunters of her time.

# Important Dates

1799—Mary Anning was born in Lyme Regis, England, on May 21.

1800—Survived a lightning strike that killed three people

1810—Death of Richard Anning, Mary's father

1811—Discovery of ichthyosaur skull by Mary's brother, Joseph Anning

1812—Found rest of ichthyosaur skeleton

1821—Another ichthyosaur found by Anning family

1823—Found first complete plesiosaur fossil

1825—Began to run family's fossil business

1828—Found rare belemnite fossil and first pterosaur in England

1829—Found second plesiosaur and chimaera fossil

1830—Found third plesiosaur

1842—Death of Mary's mother, whose name was also Mary Anning

1847—Died on March 9 of breast cancer

1848—Notice of Mary's death published in the *Quarterly Journal of the Geological Society of London.* It was the first time a nonmember was honored in this way.

# Bibliography

Conybeare, W. D. "On the Discovery of an Almost Perfect Skeleton of the
Plesiosaurus." *Transactions of the Geological Society of London* 1
(1824): 381–389.

Lang, W. D. "Mary Anning and a Very Small Boy." *Proceedings of the
Dorset Natural History and Archaeological Society* 84 (1963):
181–182.

Lang, W. D. "Mary Anning and the Fire at Lyme in 1844." *Proceedings of
the Dorset Natural History and Archaeological Society* 74 (1953):
175–177.

Lang, W. D. "Mary Anning and the Pioneer Geologists at Lyme."
*Proceedings of the Dorset Natural History and Archaeological Society*
60 (1939): 142–164.

Lang, W. D. "Mary Anning, of Lyme, Collector and Vendor of Fossils,
1799–1847." *Natural History* 5 (1936): 64–81.

Lang, W. D. "Mary Anning's Escape from Lightning." *Proceedings of the
Dorset Natural History and Archaeological Society* 80 (1959): 91–93.

Lang, W. D. "More about Mary Anning, Including a Newly-Found Letter."
*Proceedings of the Dorset Natural History and Archaeological Society*
71 (1950): 184–188.

Lang, W. D. "Portraits of Mary Anning and Other Items." *Proceedings of
the Dorset Natural History and Archaeological Society* 81 (1960):
89–91.

Lang, W. D. "Three Letters by Mary Anning, 'Fossilist,' of Lyme."
*Proceedings of the Dorset Natural History and Archaeological Society*
66 (1944): 169–173.

Taylor, Michael A., and Hugh S. Torrens. "Fossils by the Sea." *Natural
History* 104 (October 1995): 67–71.

Taylor, Michael A., and Hugh S. Torrens. "Saleswoman to a New Science."
*Proceedings of the Dorset Natural History and Archaeological Society*
108 (1987): 135–148.

Torrens, Hugh S. Correspondence with author, 1998–1999.

Torrens, Hugh S. "Presidential Address: Mary Anning (1799–1847) of
Lyme; 'the greatest fossilist the world ever knew.'" *British Journal of
the History of Science* 28 (1995): 257–284.